CATS ARE PEOPLE TOO!

CATS ARE PEOPLE TOO!

BY

P. C. VEY

A PLUME BOOK

PLUME
Published by the Penguin Group
Penguin Books USA Inc., 375 Hudson Street, New York, New York 10014, U.S.A.
Penguin Books Ltd, 27 Wrights Lane, London W8 5TZ, England
Penguin Books Australia Ltd, Ringwood, Victoria, Australia
Penguin Books Canada Ltd, 10 Alcorn Avenue, Toronto, Ontario, Canada M4V 3B2
Penguin Books (N.Z.) Ltd, 182-190 Wairau Road, Auckland 10, New Zealand

Penguin Books Ltd, Registered Offices: Harmondsworth, Middlesex, England

First published by Plume, an imprint of New American Library,
a division of Penguin Books USA Inc.

First Printing, September, 1992
10 9 8 7 6 5 4 3 2 1

 REGISTERED TRADEMARK—MARCA REGISTRADA

LIBRARY OF CONGRESS CATALOGING-IN-PUBLICATION DATA:
Vey, P. C. (Peter C.)
    Cats are people too / P.C. Vey.
      p.   cm.
    ISBN 0-452-26843-5 (pbk.)
    1. Cats—Humor.   I. Title.
  PN6231.C23V48   1992
  741.5'973—dc20   92-53542
                              CIP

Printed in the United States of America
Set in Antique Olive Light

BOOKS ARE AVAILABLE AT QUANTITY DISCOUNTS WHEN USED TO PROMOTE PRODUCTS OR SERVICES. FOR INFORMATION
PLEASE WRITE TO PREMIUM MARKETING DIVISION, PENGUIN BOOKS USA INC., 375 HUDSON STREET, NEW YORK, NEW YORK 10014.

"So, who do you want to be today?"

CAT ON A HOT TIN ROOF:
THE TRUTH REVEALED

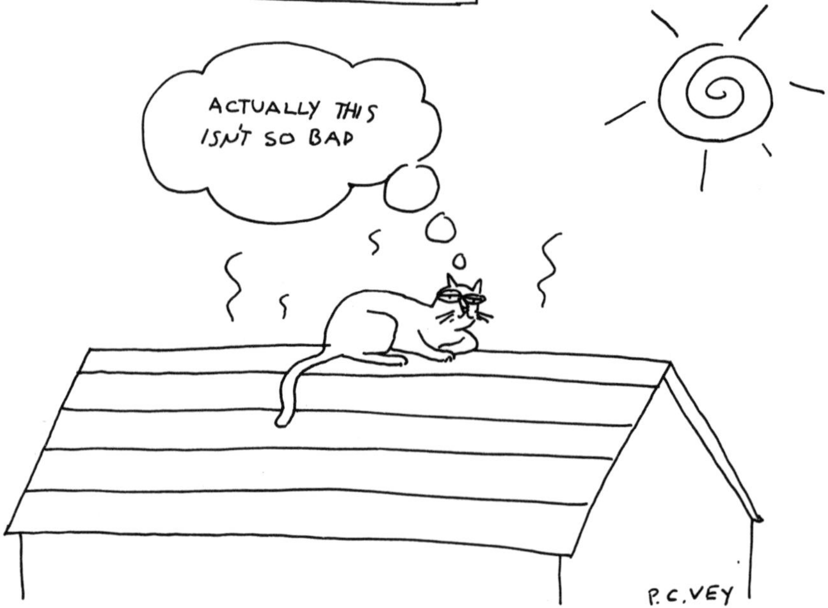

"Geez! One would think they never saw a silk upholstered eighteenth-century chaise longue ripped to shreds before!"

P.C.VEY

"What I like most about catching and killing mice is
leaving their chewed-up, dismembered bodies on the
floor for people to find."

"Honey, did a small, cute kitten with a friendly disposition always come with the evening paper?"

"I'll give you diamonds, I'll give you furs, I'll give you cat food."

But by then it was too late. Staying in the pet cargo area
had been a better idea.

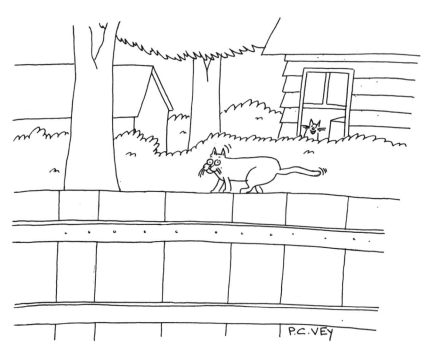

"Hey, Tom, get in here! There's a special on TV about South American tree-dwelling reptiles and forty-pound rodents that you just won't believe."

"Hey, listen, this is a strictly cash business—no bartering!"

"I can't believe kitty's being so good tonight. Usually by this time he's all over the place, ripping the furniture and drapes to shreds."

P.C. VEY

P.C.VEY

"Okay, okay . . . knock, knock . . ."

"We're only responsible for keeping them safe. If you wanted the kitty treats to stay fresh, you should have wrapped them in plastic."

"I'm not sure how the cat fits in, but without it
he gets really moody and depressed."

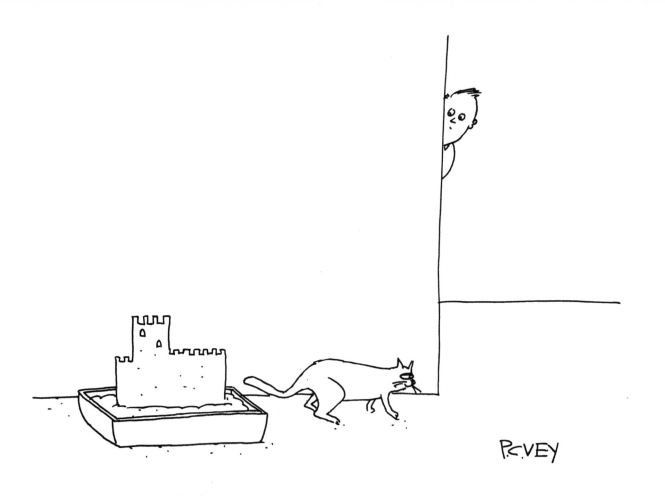

P.C. VEY

"Sorry, but with me losing my job and the raise in rent, all I could afford is bird food."

"It's his autobiography. One volume for each of his lives."

P·C·VEY

P.c.VEY

"How long has it been now since that bird moved into that tree?"

"You'll be happy to know that not only is it low in cholesterol, but it's made from free-range chicken parts."

"So, what do you plan to do with your other eight lives?"

P.C.VEY

"Well, here's your problem right here."

P.C.VEY

"... and would you mind telling our audience just how
you managed to miss such an easy jump?"

Roger's worst nightmares come true.

" . . . and where did you say you bought the cat food?"

P.C.VEY

"Oh, no, I don't want you to make him stop thinking
he's a lamp. I want you to make it work."

"You remember my son, formerly a kitten."

"That certainly was a friendly cat. Too bad we couldn't
take him home with us."

"I'll tell you what your problem is. Your problem is you don't know a good catch when you see one! Which, by the way, reminds me of the problems you had with your first wife."

"There you are!"

"Hey, pal, you have a permit to carry that thing?!"

"Brie! Nobody eats brie anymore."

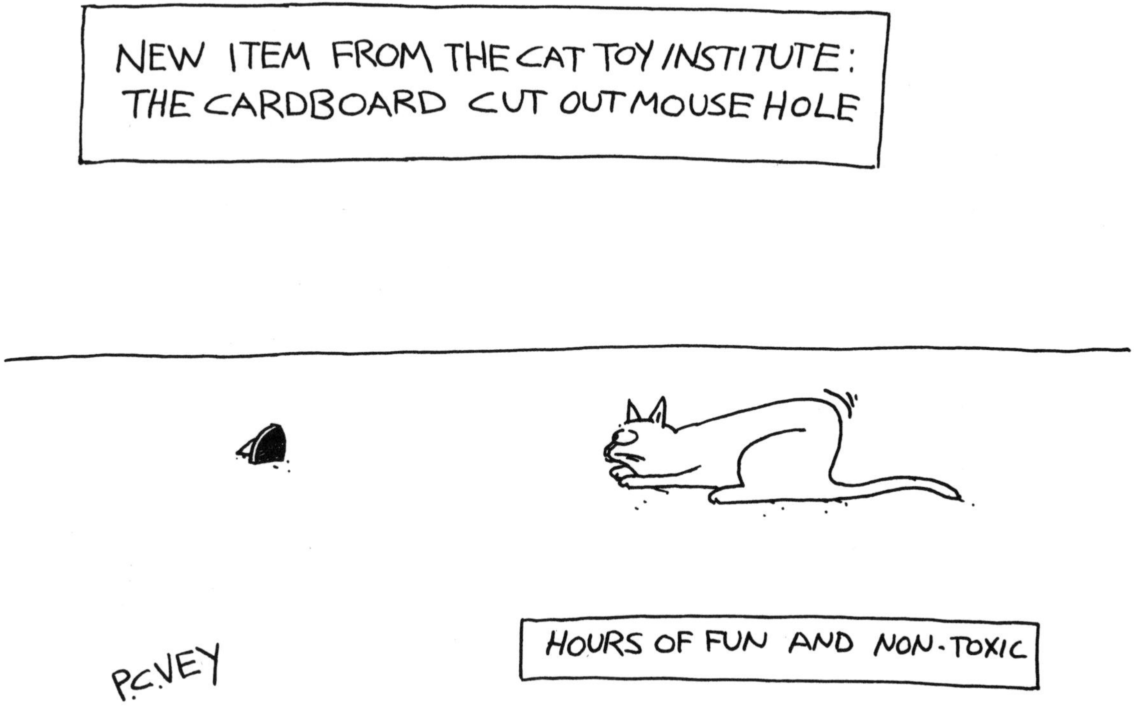
NEW ITEM FROM THE CAT TOY INSTITUTE: THE CARDBOARD CUT OUT MOUSE HOLE
HOURS OF FUN AND NON-TOXIC
P.C.VEY

"He stopped purring after three hours."

"It's a great deal. She sits on them until they hatch, and
all I have to do is fly around that dog and drive him crazy."

"Are you sure you're paying attention to him? You know nine out of ten patients recover in half the time with the comfort and love of a cat."

"I think I'll have an omelette. How about you?"

As time went on, Fluffy became increasingly finicky.

P.C.VEY

"Okay, so you're walking along, minding your own
business, when all of a sudden, for no apparent reason,
the mouse walks out of the hole and begins to bug the
heck out of you, I mean, really grating on your nerves.
You sense an urgency, a need to deal with the problem,
but you hold back, measuring your response . . ."

"He's been working with kitchen sinks and bathtubs for two years. Now he feels he's ready for the big one."

"Hey, pal, can I have some of those table scraps? You wouldn't believe how hard it is to get room service to send up table scraps."

Yet another gullible photographer falls for a typically
cruel prank by the infamous tabby twins.

"Believe me, Claudius, I would *never* serve you anything
with oat bran in it."

"Hey, pal, get your own kid."

"It's the only exercise he gets."

P.C.VEY

P.C. VEY

"Honey, did you subscribe to the Cat of the Month club?"

"... so then I thought, what the heck, let him have the darn ball of yarn. Well, little did I know ..."

"If it please the court, I just gave you a can of 'savory chicken and fish dinner' not forty-five minutes ago."

Being a suspicious cat by nature, Edward had to see for himself if he really was the most important thing in Howard's life.

"... so then he said, 'I don't see why I can't take that cat out for a walk. I mean, dogs like to go out for walks. Why not cats?'"

"Hey, listen, we don't go in for that kind of thing
around here!"

MEANWHILE, SOMEWHERE UP A TREE

P.C. VEY

"I'm not saying it isn't a great fur ball. I just don't want a fur ball, especially in trade for an egg!"

"OK, then it's decided. We'll try to get chicken and giblet donuts for the next meeting."

"You might as well take a seat. There are a couple of rubber mouse problems in front of you."

"Thickest coat I've ever seen."

"Hold all my calls, Doris. I'm going to spend some quality
time with my cat."

Tom tries out for a new home.

Three weeks later Binky goes into therapy.

"... but remember, before sauteeing the mouse, always
tenderize it by running around the room frantically with
it in your mouth and then batting it incessantly with your paw."

New cat toy

"Since when did you start counting cats to fall asleep?"

"Actually, that's not Binky. Robert took the real Binky to the summer house."

"I see something moving . . . It's a tail . . . a long, furry tail
. . . You try to catch it . . . but you can't . . It's always just
out of reach . . . You try harder and harder . . . you go
faster and faster, around and around . . . It's always just
out of reach . . . but then . . ."

"Now, what's that supposed to mean?!"

"I had no idea a whole tuna cost that much!"

"Miss Miller, a fluffy, personable cat has followed me back
from lunch. May I keep it?"

"Catwarmer."

"I just thought I ought to tell you that I'm beginning to set more realistic limits for myself, and so from now on you might find it harder to catch me."

"If I *really* want to go someplace, I just ask my mother to drive me."

"We don't care how cute you were as a kitten. You still
need an appointment to see the doctor."

"It's a pleasure to meet you. My friends tell me you're a
whiz with can openers."

P.C.VEY

"Aha! So this is why the plumber always finds hair balls in the drain pipes."

"... and, oh, one more thing. If the cat decides to sleep on my stomach tonight, could you please make him five pounds lighter?"

PLUME

PLUME TICKLES YOUR FUNNYBONE

☐ **THE UNOFFICIAL NEWLYWEDS' HANDBOOK by Alexis Magner Miller & George W. Miller (Mrs. & Mr.).** Whether you are just thinking about marriage or about to walk down the aisle—here is the one book that will keep you laughing all the way from the pre-nuptial agreement to the final mortgage payment. (266815—$7.95)

☐ **ADDICTED TO FISHING!** *A Collection of Fishing Cartoons Written Drawn, and Over-researched* **by George Peters.** From the exhilaration of catching "the Big One" to the painful realization that it is just a twenty-pound Carp, here is angler-specific humor sure to draw more laughs than a three-eyed sheephead. (266130—$5.95)

☐ **THE UNOFFICIAL NURSE'S HANDBOOK by Nina Schroeder, R.N., with Richard Mintzer.** Find out what makes a nurse tick! Nina Schroeder will have you in stitches as she introduces you to the best and worst moments in a nursing career. From favorite nurse entertainment to famous phrases they teach in nursing school, the contents of this book are guaranteed to split your sides. (258995—$7.95)

Buy them at your local bookstore or use this convenient coupon for ordering.

NEW AMERICAN LIBRARY
P.O. Box 999, Bergenfield, New Jersey 07621

Please send me the books I have checked above.
I am enclosing $_____ (please add $2.00 to cover postage and handling).
Send check or money order (no cash or C.O.D.'s) or charge by Mastercard or VISA (with a $15.00 minimum). Prices and numbers are subject to change without notice.

Card # _____ Exp. Date _____

Signature _____

Name _____

Address _____

City _____ State _____ Zip Code _____

For faster service when ordering by credit card call 1-800-253-6476

Allow a minimum of 4-6 weeks for delivery. This offer is subject to change without notice

PLUME

RIB-TICKLING BOOKS

☐ **THE UNOFFICIAL DENTIST'S HANDBOOK by Candy Schulman with illustrations by Ian Ross.** More laughs than nitrous-oxide—this hilarious book brimming with outrageous illustrations, makes an ideal gift for every practitioner and every patient who has trouble understanding what's funny about oral surgery. (265959—$7.95)

☐ **THE UNOFFICIAL MOTHER'S HANDBOOK by Norma and Art Peterson.** The essential guide for the only person who ever applauded when you went to the bathroom; the adjudicator of who hit whom first; the person known to begin sentences with "You'll be sorry when . . ." Here is an affectionately funny survey of motherhood from "day 1" through "leaving the nest" and "are you back again?" (262461—$6.95)

☐ **THE UNOFFICIAL GOLFER'S HANDBOOK by Richard Mintzer.** Step right up and tee off with this hilarious guide to the fairway—the funniest guide ever written on all the hazards of golf. (266416—$7.95)

☐ **THE JOYS OF YINGLISH by Leo Rosten.** "What a book! A celebration of scholarship, humor and linguistic anthropology."—William F. Buckley, Jr. "Open it anywhere for a laugh. Or start with *abracadabra* and work through *zlob* for an education and endless amusement."—*Booklist* (265436—$14.95)

Prices slightly higher in Canada.

Buy them at your local bookstore or use this convenient coupon for ordering.

NEW AMERICAN LIBRARY
P.O. Box 999, Bergenfield, New Jersey 07621

Please send me the books I have checked above.
I am enclosing $_____ (please add $2.00 to cover postage and handling).
Send check or money order (no cash or C.O.D.'s) or charge by Mastercard or VISA (with a $15.00 minimum). Prices and numbers are subject to change without notice.

Card # _____ Exp. Date _____

Signature _____

Name _____

Address _____

City _____ State _____ Zip Code _____

For faster service when ordering by credit card call 1-800-253-6476

Allow a minimum of 4-6 weeks for delivery. This offer is subject to change without notice

IT'S RAINING CATS AND DOGS